What Our Readers Have Said...

"Although I consider myself a seasoned sales professional, it is helpful to have past learning's refreshed. The books were also beneficial because of the information concerning 'trends' in the sales relationship. The sales process should be viewed as dynamic since business relationships change regularly."

•

"For the particular business I am in and the type of sales calls I have, I find that the books in the Pinpoint Sales Training Series are very often applicable to how I conduct business. I would recommend them to other sales people, just not ones that are in my industry."

•

"These books provide very good concepts. It fits in well with the Bell Leadership training program that I attended in November."

•

"I use this material in these books and apply it to my customers and other employees I work with."

•

"I would like to know other topics. Is there anything on Production Management or Consultative Selling or Time Management?"

•

"These books are great tools that should be used as guidelines for our everyday

supervisory practices. You need to take the time to do a short self-evaluation when reading them."

•

"The Pinpoint Training Series delivers information that could be used in a lot different areas."

•

"I like this because I can take them with me to read at a convenient time. I feel the little time I have to spend in the office is best use on activities that directly relate to revenue opportunities. I like the short amount of time it takes to keep up with these."

•

"I prefer the self-study approach; it fits in with my schedule."

•

"My thought is that the real value of these books comes into effect when doing the action plans."

•

"Short and sweet. These books are easy to comprehend."

•

"I have enjoyed reading these books. They are relevant to today's work environment and the ongoing change in the way we manage our workforce."

•

"I do feel that these books have been very helpful to me at my job."

•

"I think a lot of the recommendations in these books are very useful, and can be applicable to everyday situations. If nothing else, it's a good reference guide to fall back upon if a situation arises in the future."

•

"These books are relevant to today's work environment and the ongoing change in the way we manage our workforce."

•

Large Accounts Sales & Management Strategies

Pinpoint Sales Skill Development Training Series

TIMOTHY F. BEDNARZ

MAJORIUM
BUSINESS PRESS

Pinpoint Sales Skill Development Training Series
"Large Account Sales & Management Strategies"
Timothy F. Bednarz

Graphic design: Monika Pawlak

Majorium Business Press
2025 Main Street
Stevens Point, WI 54481
715.342.1018 • 800.654.4935

ISBN 978-1-882181-94-0

Printed in the United States of America

Introduction

The Pinpoint Sales Skill Development Training Series is designed for targeted training and education regarding increased improvement in a specific skill or competency.

Each book within this series is designed to be easy to use, understand and apply to your job. It can be used as a basis for training individuals, as a discussion guide or as a personal training tool.

Each chapter within this book discusses a specific concept. When you have completed all eight chapters you should have a 360° perspective of the topic.

Additionally, each chapter is divided into specific sections:

- The first section provides you with an overview of the topic
- The Implications section discusses why the concept is important, and why it is important to learn and apply.
- The Strategies, Tips & Techniques to Apply section teaches how to use and apply the particular concept to your work.
- The Points to Ponder section gives you something to think about or to be discussed with a group setting. These are questions not meant to be immediately answered, but to be pondered over time.
- The Training Activity section provides you with the tools to transfer what you have learned to your job. It is designed to help create an action plan to effectively apply the concept.

Each of the topics in this series is time-tested and proven in the marketplace. They have been used by thousands of employees as training tools. Many of the users have commented that what made these books valuable, was the ability to refer to them when a problem surfaced. They indicated that they remembered reading about the exact problem. They referred back to these books and found an appropriate solution.

You will find them equally valuable as a resource in your professional development library.

Table of Contents

LEARNING OBJECTIVES:

- Essential strategies for establishing, building and monitoring large accounts.
- How to identify, gather and manage large account information.
- How to keep large accounts from becoming jeopardized.
- How to eliminate inconsistencies in account planning practices, structures and procedures.
- How to create a comprehensive, formalized account statement for targeted accounts.
- Ways to establish and maintain relationships with large account decision makers.
- Methods and practices to counter large account competition.
- How to position offerings and support from a large account's viewpoint.
- How to determine realistic goals and revenue streams.

1

Large Account Management Takes Teamwork

Inconsistent and ineffective account management—especially for larger accounts—is more common in today's organizations. Salespeople, managers and companies as a whole need to develop and employ specific strategies allowing all directly and indirectly involved organizational members to assume responsibility, oversight and control over key accounts and their related activities. Within today's competitive environment, employing a team approach is essential if large accounts are to be retained as stable and reliable company assets.

IMPLICATIONS – WHAT THIS MEANS TO YOU

As part of the initial process, the first item to consider is which particular members within an organization need to be included as essential component parts of a large account management team. Account relationship functions must be carefully considered and weighed before placing individuals into specific team roles. The more input solicited from these selected individuals, the more reliable resulting account analyses, decision making and retention strategies become.

Typical large account management teams are often comprised of salespeople who are directly responsible for selling and handling particular existing or targeted accounts, branch or division managers, customer service people, market research individuals and any others who have any role to fill in terms of network support functions. As research indicates, the size or function of account teams is not as important as the commitments made by the individual members within them to generate successful outcomes.

A large account team also includes at least one and usually two designated personal account representatives. These individuals are assigned to the team because they are able to offer valuable input and updated information regarding various changes and transformations that are occurring within the company itself. This includes such things as new need requirements and transitions in operation methods. These insights are vital for establishing proper internal oversight procedures and implementing proactive management changes.

Team meeting time frames can vary. A management team must be given a wide range of flexibility. All individuals do not have to be present at the same time or at the same location in order to plan strategies. The key is for all members to be willing to provide information, analyses, input and suggestions as needed to other team members who deal directly with the larger account(s) on a regular basis.

The main benefit of applying a team approach to large account management is sharing responsibilities and accountability. Another benefit is found in the synergy that the process itself creates, which tends to improve customer responsiveness. Larger accounts can see their best interests and top priorities being paid close attention to, from salespeople and top-level managers, down to account and support level departments. Success is built upon total company-wide ongoing involvement that becomes visually recognized.

STRATEGIES, TIPS & TECHNIQUES TO APPLY

A proactive diagnosis is intended to uncover hidden account-related problems and issues. Nothing is worse than having to operate in "damage control mode" where team members are taken off guard due to hidden factors that necessitate altering direction of the team's strategic action plans. Without conducting a proactive diagnosis it is easy to have some problems get out of control, which in turn makes managing the account much more difficult, stressful and time-consuming.

There are five important elements to address when conducting a proactive diagnosis.

Determining Existing Inconsistencies

The first step in conducting a proactive diagnosis is to determine inconsistencies in account planning practices, structures and procedures that have been experienced in various territorial or regional units. This implies determining how various units, divisions and departments tend to (or not to) operate as collective entities. Analyzing these without documenting their linkages renders the process useless.

Information—gathered and analyzed from future and past sales data—needs to identify exactly what was sold to the various accounts within the last several years. Most often the optimal way to determine this information is to break sales data down by product line and the particular divisions selling them (in other words, the part(s) of the company the accounts actually did business with). Business plan forecasts can help determine current and fairly accurate estimates of projected sales.

Account Strategy Analyses

Linkages between current account strategies and the revenue larger accounts are generating must be detailed and well documented. It is also necessary to identify just how these large accounts grew to their current sizes. This can be accomplished by addressing the various factors and variables that came into play in their growth process. Defining time factors in terms of planning and monitoring and how each influenced the evolution of the accounts also needs to be addressed.

The key is to make certain that that all adopted account strategies work to positively impact company bottom-line revenues.

Measuring and Monitoring Procedures

It is essential to determine whether or not current account plans are working, and equally important to know how soon this information is available. Frequency of account tracking as a major objective should never be minimized or ignored. If predetermined account plan goals are too broad, vague, unrealistic, or off-course, they must be revisited and redefined. Midcourse corrections are the hardest to develop strategies for and implement, as account damage is often far too advanced. This in turn makes effective recovery procedures reactive rather than proactive.

Reviewing and Detailing Account Budgets

It is essential to identify the level of company account plan resources. When analyzing various accounts, expected returns on investment need to be detailed. All targeted or existing accounts should warrant the needed resources to maintain, sustain and grow them.

Information Gathering and Management

Effective account strategies are never developed in a void. In reality they are nothing more than proactive actions developed from analyzed, managed and culled "usable" information, including:

- All data that discloses what has been directly and indirectly sold to customers;
- Data that reflects business and industry trends;
- Data that discloses changes in business environments;
- Data that aids in detailing customer account threats and opportunities;
- Data that indicates account profit losses or gains;
- Data that indicates where operations are anticipated to expand and why;
- Information that can detail particular facts that help identify what influences each account;
- Information that can detail particular facts to help the sales organization increase each account's profitability and productivity.

POINTS TO PONDER — SOMETHING TO THINK ABOUT

1. Have you ever felt that from a company-wide perspective, large accounts are being jeopardized?
2. Do you feel you are personally able to take adequate care of your large accounts? Why or why not?

TRAINING ACTIVITY — APPLICATION & ACTION PLAN

1. From a personal sales standpoint or from a team perspective, analyze the following account procedures. Identify whether or not they are effective functions within your organization.
   - Determining Existing Inconsistencies
   - Account Strategy Analyses
   - Measuring and Monitoring Procedures
   - Reviewing and Detailing Account Budgets
   - Information Gathering and Management
2. If any weaknesses exist, determine how certain methods or procedures can be improved. Identify what is needed to more effectively maintain large account coverage for better retention and increased sales.

2

Setting the Stage for Analyzing Large Accounts

Account strategies need to be based on properly and effectively managed business-related data. Strategies developed are only as good as the pertinent and usable documented data and information that is gleaned and collected.

IMPLICATIONS – WHAT THIS MEANS TO YOU

To be able to effectively manage important business-related data, it is necessary to become sensitized to feelings of uncertainty or uneasiness in regard to what is going on in any particular large account. These internal feelings of discomfort should be considered "caution flags" signaling the possibility that the account may be in jeopardy and headed to a high risk category.

Intuition is one of the most reliable indicators signaling the need to gather more proactive, insightful account information. When something does not "feel quite right" about what is happening within a certain large account, steps can be taken to reveal hidden problems before they can damage company relationships and account stability.

STRATEGIES, TIPS & TECHNIQUES TO APPLY

When beginning the process of gathering more information to manage an account successfully, it is wise to begin with a single high risk account where pertinent information seems to be incomplete, unclear or omitted. Analyzing various areas of the account plan information to pinpoint just what particular data, factors or insights may be missing will be highly productive in terms of generating positive end results to keep the account alive and active. The process also allows the account team and salespeople to gain valuable insights and perspectives as to the "ins and outs" of the analyses and disclosing processes themselves.

In starting the process, all forms of pertinent, usable information are collected in order to get a better handle on the account and where it appears to be heading and why, as well as specific industry-related data directly pertaining to the particular roles account team members take.

Each designated individual needs to extract only the exact amount of pertinent, usable information needed to help establish a more solid footing to define where the company account is or should be going as current identified trends tend to indicate. Process changes in the company's market environment and general business climate must be identified, addressed, and linked to the account's overall major concerns, market threats, opportunities, strengths, weaknesses, desires and established mission statement.

It is essential to consider trend or expansion issues in relationship to what the sales company can take advantage of and comfortably provide. This implies understanding shrinking or enhanced profits and where the account's growth potential appears to reside. This type of information can be obtained from several sources, one being personal company sales-related facts, forecasts, reports and figures.

One of the most important pieces of information to cull is a realistic projection in regard to the account's future sales. It is a must to review and analyze accounting reports, including current and annual past corporate reports and stockholder briefings.

Product-related literature and brochures or ads generally offer helpful insights into an account's general positioning, targeted customers and strength within the market. This information is essential for actual strategy planning and goal setting. Data needs to be analyzed to determine the account's overall health in terms of financial strength.

If the company is publicly traded, its overall viability must be determined. Television or print media, journal reports, news programs or stockholder interviews can help disclose this type of information, even though some may be biased. The best places to begin searching for this information are public libraries, business bookstores, university libraries or resource centers, and the Internet.

It is important to determine whether the information collected can be confirmed as being reliable, realistic and accurate. As internal organizational "champions" are excellent resources to rely on when it comes to verifying current or previously collected information, salespeople should find one or more individuals within the account who understand the total workings of the company and how it functions and operates. These individuals should have good existing rapport with (or be open to developing relationships with) other account team members.

When talking to contacts, salespeople need to gain perspectives on negative information as well as selective, positive insights. Even though some types of information may not be what salespeople desire to hear, it is necessary to obtain it. Negative insights can work to enhance particular strategies rather than short-circuiting them when it comes to planning, establishing and implementing directional courses of action.

Once comprehensive information is gathered and confirmed, it is important that all account team members understand how the sales company is positioned within the particular account, as well as how the account is positioned within the marketplace environment.

Market concerns, business-related issues and current trends must be weighed and prioritized in order to determine just how the sales company and customer account will be able to work together to meet specified goals and objectives.

When large accounts are properly analyzed, the process makes the best use of financial capital and human resources, as well as company-related time and effort in relationship to both parties.

POINTS TO PONDER — SOMETHING TO THINK ABOUT

1. What types of information do you currently find yourself gathering to help understand your large targeted accounts' methods of operations and placements within current business markets and environments?
2. Do you have a current account team that you can rely upon to help gather some pertinent and necessary information for particular accounts?

TRAINING ACTIVITY — APPLICATION & ACTION PLAN

Identify one account that you consider to be at risk. Get a better handle on the account by doing the following:

1. If possible, select several members that can help gather necessary information from an account team standpoint.
2. Make certain that each gathers only the information needed from the particular role perspective within one selected account.
3. Gain perspectives on negative related information as well as positive insights, with the understanding that both are necessary for developing appropriate strategies, goals and objectives.
4. Make use of public libraries, business bookstores, university libraries or resource centers and the Internet when seeking out information and data.
5. Utilize company account "champions" for verifying and double-checking currently or previously culled information.
6. Identify changes in the company's market environment and general business climate.

7. Link this information to the account's overall major concerns, market threats, opportunities, strengths, weaknesses, desires and established mission statement.
8. Consider trend or expansion issues in relation to what the sales company can take advantage of by examining the account's shrinking or enhanced profits and where its growth potential lies.

3

Beginning the Process from an Account's Point of View

Large accounts need vast amounts of dedication, understanding and effort to be well served. Such an effort begins with an understanding of how a particular large account views the salesperson, as well as their total support system, including their account team.

IMPLICATIONS — WHAT THIS MEANS TO YOU

Part of the process of managing large accounts requires bringing hidden problems to the surface before they jeopardize them. Conducting a preventative analysis, including an intensive diagnosis of procedures and shortcomings, should become a top priority.

STRATEGIES, TIPS & TECHNIQUES TO APPLY

Determining Existing Inconsistencies

The first step in conducting a proactive diagnosis is to determine inconsistencies in account planning practices, structures and procedures that have been experienced in various territorial or regional units. This implies determining how various units, divisions and departments tend to (or not to) operate as collective entities. Analyzing these without documenting their linkages renders the process useless.

Information—gathered and analyzed from future and past sales data—needs to identify exactly what was sold to the various accounts within the last several years. Most often the optimal way to determine this information is to break sales data down by product line and the particular divisions selling them (in other words, the part(s) of the company the accounts actually did business with). Business plan forecasts can help determine current and fairly accurate estimates of projected sales.

Account Strategy Analyses

Linkages between current account strategies and the revenue larger accounts are generating must be detailed and well documented. It is also necessary to identify just how these large accounts grew to their current sizes. This can be accomplished by addressing the various factors and variables that came into play in their growth process. Defining time factors in terms of planning and monitoring and how each influenced the evolution of the accounts also needs to be addressed.

The key is to make certain that all adopted account strategies work to positively impact company bottom-line revenues.

Measuring and Monitoring Procedures

It is essential to determine whether or not current account plans are working, and equally important to know how soon this information is available. Frequency of account tracking as a major objective should never be minimized or ignored. If predetermined account plan goals are too broad, vague, unrealistic, or off-course, they must be revisited and redefined. Midcourse corrections are the hardest to develop strategies for and implement, as account damage is often far too advanced. This in turn makes effective recovery procedures reactive rather than proactive.

Reviewing and Detailing Account Budgets

It is essential to identify the level of company account plan resources. When analyzing various accounts, expected returns on investment need to be detailed. All targeted or existing accounts should warrant the needed resources to maintain, sustain and grow them.

Information Gathering and Management

Effective account strategies are never developed in a void. In reality they are nothing more than proactive actions developed from analyzed, managed and culled "usable" information, including:

- All data that discloses what has been directly and indirectly sold to customers;
- Data that reflects business and industry trends;
- Data that discloses changes in business environments;
- Data that aids in detailing customer account threats and opportunities;
- Data that indicates account profit losses or gains;
- Data that indicates where operations are anticipated to expand and why;
- Information that can detail particular facts that help identify what influences each account;
- Information that can detail particular facts to help the sales organization increase each account's profitability and productivity.

POINTS TO PONDER — SOMETHING TO THINK ABOUT

1. Have you ever felt that from a company-wide perspective, large accounts are being jeopardized?
2. Do you feel you are personally able to take adequate care of your large accounts? Why or why not?

TRAINING ACTIVITY — APPLICATION & ACTION PLAN

1. From a personal sales standpoint or from a team perspective, analyze the following account procedures.
2. Identify whether or not they are effective functions within your organization.
    - Determining Existing Inconsistencies
    - Account Strategy Analyses
    - Measuring and Monitoring Procedures
    - Reviewing and Detailing Account Budgets
    - Information Gathering and Management
3. If any weaknesses exist, determine how certain methods or procedures can be improved. Identify what is needed to more effectively maintain large account coverage for better retention and increased sales.

4

Establishing an Account Statement

An account statement works to define the basic direction in which salespeople or account teams need to proceed for individually identified large account segments. Focusing in on one particular account-related segment, it is intended to define where selective products or services will fit most appropriately.

IMPLICATIONS – WHAT THIS MEANS TO YOU

Today's typical large accounts tend to be in the practice of subdividing or merging in order to grow and gain market share strength. These segmented outgrowths tend to all have differing needs, efficiency factors, and productivity and functioning requirements, and are focused, operated, controlled and managed completely separately from one another. As such, salespeople can never expect to sell the same way to all of them, and attempting to match similar products or services will be impossible.

Unrelated business issues and specific major concerns will need to be overcome on an individual basis. The best place to begin is to define one specific area to focus on that can be suitably cultivated and effectively managed. Account statements are intended to put these elements into a thoroughly defined, well-written, documented format.

STRATEGIES, TIPS & TECHNIQUES TO APPLY

Problems can be expected to occur within large account selling. Salespeople end up offering products or services for widely defined segments rather than one particular, but compatible, portion within their selective accounts. Predetermined strategies generally become far too vague and unclear to be effective. When this happens, salespeople generally end up attempting to sell products or services to entirely inappropriate segments, which generally results in muddling the sales focus and wasting the time, energy and effort of both parties.

Constructing account statements works to help eliminate these kinds of hindering situations.

To create a comprehensive, formalized account statement for each targeted account, three vital questions need to be addressed and answered. The first is, "What particular segment of the total large account are we as a company selling to, or should we be selling to?"

To help define this portion of the account statement, it is essential to define what particular types of customers the account segment is selling to. It is also essential to identify and define the general products or services being provided within the total segmented market.

The number of divisions and departments it has must be determined and analyzed for similar product or service offering compatibility. Rather than trying to sell too broadly, it is much more effective to work on one targeted portion of the total account as an individual major goal.

The second question that needs to be asked is, "What particular products or services will best match each specific segment and meet its particular needs, business operation requirements, and most pressing concerns?"

A starting point is to define the total playing field of one targeted company and analyze what problems or concerns are of major importance within a given segment. It should then be determined how to tie in particular products or services to exact customer problems.

To help instill a sense of value, salespeople should think in terms of what customers believe each product or service will be able to do for them and why, as well as the contributions the company and offering(s) can provide, such as time, technology capabilities and cost savings. The specific problems that will be addressed should be spelled out together with the best possible solutions.

The third question becomes, "What value and benefits can be provided to the account that will be difficult to match or duplicate?" It is helpful to think in terms of profit generated results and ways to document them, such as:

- Increasing sales
- Lowering overall costs
- Increasing productivity
- Providing ongoing services
- Ease of use
- Eliminating redundancies in procedures or operations

Once this information is obtained, responses can be generated into a written account statement that can then be used to identify an effective sales strategy that will not get bogged down with irrelevant message content or details that fail to address specific needs. Once written, consensus on the wording should be reached before a final draft is created.

POINTS TO PONDER — SOMETHING TO THINK ABOUT

1. Have you ever found yourself offering products or services for widely defined segments rather than one particular, but compatible, portion within a large account?
2. To help define a sense of value in regard to your individual offerings, do you normally think in terms of what customers believe each product or service will be able to do for them and why?

TRAINING ACTIVITY — APPLICATION & ACTION PLAN

Write down answers to the following questions, then combine responses with other account team members to develop a complete, focused account statement.

1. What particular segment of the total large account are we as a company selling to, or should we be, and why?
2. What particular product(s) or service(s) will offer the best match for each specific segment of a company I am working with, to effectively meet its particular needs, business operation requirements, and major concerns?
3. What value and benefits can I as a salesperson, and we collectively as an account team and company, provide to the account that will be difficult to match or duplicate?
4. Why will these things be difficult to compete with?
5. How can they be successfully positioned?

5

Securing High Level Relationships

Establishing a large account implies having a relationship with its inclusive decision making members. In order to be solidly forged and enduring, relationship building needs to be professional, business-focused and personal.

How associations are built and the effort that goes into establishing a relationship becomes the major differentiating factor between creating a flimsy partnership that is easily uprooted, or one that is steadfast. A solid, cemented relationship is considered to be one that can sustain itself through uncomfortable or negative issues, concerns and problems.

IMPLICATIONS – WHAT THIS MEANS TO YOU

The high end of the purchaser-vendor relationship process is the most desirable position to be in, whereas the worst place to be is where salespeople or account teams are viewed as simply supplying various undifferentiated commodities.

Most salespeople or account teams find themselves somewhere in the middle of these two positions: they are perceived to supply what is considered to be "good" or "high-quality" products or services. However, a middle positioning generally means having to deal with the most amount of competition.

It is essential to understand the purchaser-vendor relationship in terms of levels of positioning within a large account. Knowing the specific level a salesperson or account team occupies within the buy-sell relationship process becomes valuable, usable knowledge.

The customer or account determines the exact level at which a salesperson is positioned.

If the customer or account perceives that the salesperson falls at a lower level, it is essential to begin attempting to work upward within the buy-sell perceptual layers. Once again, it is the customer or account that decides how effective these efforts are.

Creating Higher Positioning Through Value

Salespeople need to ensure better positioning in today's service intensive and sensitive economy. As providing more than is normally expected becomes one major way to differentiate their offerings, it is essential to provide good quality products or services as well as reliable support in the total offering package.

Today, service and support are beginning to replace features and benefits as major selling points. Thus it is essential to become committed to "making things happen." This implies making a good impression by following through on what is promised in order to demonstrate dependability, accountability and reliability.

Provide Help in Running the Large Account's Business

When selling to a large account to become positioned higher within the purchaser-vendor hierarchy, it becomes essential to understand its business goals and objectives. It also becomes essential to comprehend its problems, both externally and internally. In order to add value by offering professional insight and assistance, sales people and account teams need to:

- Generate ideas for addressing and solving day-to-day problems and operational needs.

- Generate ideas as to how to improve company profitability.
- Develop and present solutions for only upper-level concerns and priorities.
- Think long term to obtain continuous repeat business.
- Identify and define pragmatic, cost-effective solutions designed to meet exact needs, or ones that can grow with anticipated ongoing business improvements or development.

Develop Non-Business Solutions Not Directly Related to the Account's Sales Proposal

Differentiation by generating alternative non-business solutions is one effective way to increase purchaser-vendor hierarchy positioning.

Solutions generated for bottom-line problems, issues and concerns do not always have to be directly related to what is typically included within a sales proposal. These generally complex solutions often exceed what a sales company does or represents and what is typically expected of it to do.

Alternative business solutions, on the other hand, are defined as providing expertise in planning, design, guidance and direction in a manner that provides abstract and divergent supportive services for the large account. As a vendor, it may be possible to offer needed assistance as a service that can help generate improvements or methods for overcoming pressing external customer needs and demands.

For instance, some companies may appreciate help in overcoming low employee productivity, in which case as a vendor it may be possible to establish and offer an employee assistance program to address issues and ways to motivate and improve employee performance.

In another example, some companies have numerous divisions or need to rely on other retail company counterparts to keep business operations and sales flowing smoothly. As a vendor it may be well worthwhile to consider hosting focus groups or meetings by bringing various groups together to smooth out existing frustrations, problems or issues. Solutions like these immediately instill upper level purchaser-vendor positioning due to the vendor's creative actions, abilities and sophistication.

POINTS TO PONDER — SOMETHING TO THINK ABOUT

1. What level of positioning do you feel you are at most of the time within large accounts? Why?
2. Do you make it a priority to understand your large accounts' problems, both externally and internally, as well as their business goals and objectives?

TRAINING ACTIVITY — APPLICATION & ACTION PLAN

To help establish high level positioning within your large accounts, define and determine how you can:

1. Identify what placement and positioning you tend to hold in regard to the purchaser-vendor relationship from each large account's point of view.
2. Go the extra mile to increase your chances for higher positioning in the purchaser-vendor relationship hierarchy.
3. Go about developing solutions that meet upper level concerns and priorities.
4. Go beyond the boundaries that exceed what your company typically does or represents and what is normally expected of it to do.
5. Begin to identify and consider possible ways to provide expertise in planning, design, guidance and direction in a manner that provides abstract and divergent supportive services.

6

Compiling Large Account Information

It is essential to carefully appraise large account situations by viewing things through the minds and eyes of large account customers. In order to generate higher levels of receptivity, it is essential to see things in just the same way the decision makers and support people do within each large account. Receptivity is structured around the way each company sees the world they need to function within: internally, externally, geographically and globally.

IMPLICATIONS — WHAT THIS MEANS TO YOU

Salespeople need to develop better positioning by providing numerous, specific benefits that are directly linked to the offering. Better positioning is also achieved by identifying and defining how the company and its offering is able to help the large account better deal with competitors, market ups and downs, and/or internal and external problems. Without doing this, salespeople will never be able to position themselves beyond the initial starting gate.

STRATEGIES, TIPS & TECHNIQUES TO APPLY

Salespeople and account teams must first begin the information-gathering process by identifying and defining how each large account can benefit by utilizing their company. This includes:

Understanding How Large Accounts View Their Functioning World

To understand how large account customers think and perceive their worlds, it is important to begin addressing each account separately in areas such as:

- Its general state stability or instability;
- How its management is structured;
- Its problems and opportunities;
- Its organization, profit and loss performance, and the market forces it is experiencing, including major and minor competition;
- Its various departmental operations and smoothness of workflow as well as particular glitches or associated problems or slowdowns;
- Its strategic management as well as departmental concerns, issues and priorities;
- Its various types of internal agendas, turf battles and conflicting missions or visions.

All of the above factors affect how decisions are influenced, addressed and made, and must be weighed, analyzed and defined from all decision makers' and, oftentimes, employees' perspectives.

Developing Answers to Focused Questions

As the above information is developed, a concerted effort must be made to address the following questions from customer viewpoints, which include:

- What is the overall situation this particular large account is facing?
- What can we as a company do and offer to help?
- Does this large account fully understand the industry we are in, and if not how can we define it effectively, simply and from its point of view?
- How does the large account view the competition our company is facing?
- Where do they see us in terms of our positioning and why?
- How does the large account view our company as a whole?

- How does it view us as compared to other vendors?
- Are there areas that are harder to identify and define in regard to what they think or feel about us? How can these areas be successfully revealed?
- How much should we involve the customer members in the account planning process?
- How much and what type of customer input will help to better position our company and offering?

Identifying How Large Accounts View Your Offering's Place Within Their Purchasing Structure

Special emphasis must be placed on each large account's general purchasing practices. It is essential to understand how an offering can be better positioned by adapting or modifying it to meet specific large account needs.

The following questions must be answered:

- What is each large account's purchasing philosophy?
- Does it tend to remain loyal to one vendor?
- Are there any trends or pattern changes in what is purchased and how? For example, does it spread its purchases throughout the year, or does it purchase at very selective times in larger quantities?
- What are the account's primary purchasing and selection criteria? Does it look more at price or value?
- How much flexibility does it have in terms of specification requirements?
- How much importance is placed on product specifications, availability and extras like service support, service capabilities or delivery times?
- Who are all the major players in the decision making chain? Who are the influencers? Who else will have an impact on the decision making process?
- Are there any variations within departments? Who are the final approvers within them?

- Who are the individuals who maintain the most control over final purchasing approval?
- Does the large account appear to have a predetermined attitude toward our company as to how it fits into their industry? Does it appear to project that it desires a mutual partnership that is beneficial for both parties?

Once all these questions have been addressed and detailed, the information can be used to develop a more strategic sales presentation. This will greatly help to enhance not only the salesperson's image, but also his or her offering's differentiation as well as overall positioning.

POINTS TO PONDER — SOMETHING TO THINK ABOUT

1. Do you analyze how your offering can be better positioned by adapting or modifying it to meet specific large account needs?
2. What types of questions do you normally ask to comprehend how customers within large accounts view the worlds in which they function?

TRAINING ACTIVITY — APPLICATION & ACTION PLAN

To help develop a more strategic sales presentation or message that helps define your offering's differentiation and improves your overall positioning, address and detail the following questions.

- What elements define the overall situation that this particular large account is facing?
- What can we effectively do to help its situation?
- From a customer perspective, what other questions are necessary to ask and answer that have not been addressed within this lesson?

- Is there an understanding as to each large account's general purchasing practices?
- Is there any more information that needs to be gathered?
- How can all this information be successfully tied into a sales message or presentation in order to better differentiate and position my offering?

7

Countering the Competition

An avid competitor is the greatest threat to securing a sale. As such, it is critical to identify who the salesperson and their company is competing against, and why. Furthermore, because customers—not salespeople—are the best judges of who their competitors are and why, it is important to get a fix on how each large account views the competitive situation.

IMPLICATIONS – WHAT THIS MEANS TO YOU

It is important to determine how the large account feels about existing competitors as compared to the salesperson and their company. An extremely subjective area, the only way to acquire this information is to openly ask the members within the account.

There are basic areas that large accounts tend to use as criteria to weigh and measure one competitor against another. It is important to identify just what areas of strength salespeople hold and areas where the competition appears to have the upper hand.

The areas large account customers typically measure include:

- Levels of trust, accountability and integrity;
- The depth of the existing relationship;
- In-depth comprehension of the large account's business situation and problems;
- Product or service match that is able to best meet the large account's needs and requirements;

- Levels of positioning with the large account;
- Value and pricing;
- Overall care and concern for what happens within the account to help attain its objectives and goals.

STRATEGIES, TIPS & TECHNIQUES TO APPLY

Positioning themselves more favorably in the eyes of large accounts by looking for competitive voids and gaps needs to become a primary concern for all salespeople.

Conduct a Gap Assessment

The first step in achieving a more favorable position is to conduct an assessment to subjectively rate how the salesperson's company is doing within the account. Salespeople need to ask several questions of themselves, their company and the large account to complete this process. Though the responses are subjective, they will help determine possible areas of weakness as well as strengths.

- How well is the large account doing within its particular market and existing territories and its industry as a whole? –The answer to this question will reveal just what opportunities exist for future business with the account.
- How fast or slow is the large account's business growing? Is it stagnant or flourishing? Does its growth pattern offer any selling advantage? –These answers will help determine how effectively the salesperson's company capabilities will be assimilated into the large account's growth and expansion.
- Do members of the large account appear to trust my company, the total account team, and me enough to use our professional expertise, advice and instruction? –The answer to this question determines whether members of the account are truly interested and invested in what the salesperson is able to offer and provide in terms of resulting solutions.

- Do I feel uplifted when working with account members? –This question reveals whether or not a solid relationship has been established, where both parties feel a sense of mutual benefit and gain from the process. Salespeople can further detail what they like and dislike about working with the account and why.
- Could I obtain a good reference from the large account? –If salespeople believe they wouldn't be able to get a good written reference or other company referral, or would be afraid to ask for one, the bonds of partnership need to be reexamined.

Conduct a Gap Assessment from the Large Account's Point of View

The following questions should be answered from the large account's point of view:

- Can I rely on this company to provide whatever needs or requirements I may have?
- How well is the company measuring up in its particular market and existing territories and its industry as a whole?
- Is this vendor growing or is it stagnant or floundering?
- Does this particular vendor offer any advantages or benefits that other competitors can't?
- Is there an existing sense of trust in the salesperson (or account team) and their company?
- What elements do members of this company feel define a sense of partnership as well as workable relationship?
- Can my large company depend on this vendor to provide useful and beneficial professional expertise, advice and instruction?
- Do the members of my decision making team feel comfortable and secure with the salesperson and his or her company?
- Has my company received good reports about the vendor company's ethics, levels of support, ability to provide exceptional value, and quality products/services or capabilities that go beyond what is normally anticipated or expected?

Compare Viewpoints

Analyzing the responses requires distilling critical information and comparing and placing some type of scoring structure to the process. Salespeople should begin by comparing and contrasting answers from their own and the large account's perspective to each question.

Such an analysis will help the salesperson determine if they may be pushing too hard or not hard enough in pursuing the account, and whether the relationship process needs to be cemented more solidly. They should also analyze just what contributions they can make to the large account's bottom line that has not already been introduced, acknowledged or discussed.

POINTS TO PONDER — SOMETHING TO THINK ABOUT

1. When working with a large account, do you make it a point to look for competitive gaps?
2. Can you identify the basic areas that each of your large accounts use as criteria to weigh and measure you against other competitors?

TRAINING ACTIVITY — APPLICATION & ACTION PLAN

Weigh and measure each separate large account's viewpoint against your own:

1. Discuss as a team what any discrepancies imply.
2. Determine reasons why they may exist.
3. Define ways to revisit weaker areas from the questions that had a negative response.
4. Identify ways to improve the account relationship as well as possible company or offering capabilities.

8

Determining Realistic Revenue Streams and Related Goals

Conducting a situational appraisal is one of the most effective ways to begin identifying realistic revenue streams. Sound strategies involve capitalizing on strengths by focusing them directly on available opportunities and pairing them in a way that offers higher levels of revenue potential.

Every strength identified needs to become part of the large account strategy, including the defining of realistic overall revenue goals with all involved parties having a direct role within the sales as well as account management and maintenance processes.

IMPLICATIONS — WHAT THIS MEANS TO YOU

In large account selling it is essential to set quantitative goals that directly correlate to the revenue streams each separate account should generate. Intended to be accurate indicators of expected volume, primary revenue targets become the necessary hard data that support all selling efforts and realistic appraisals as to whether or not an account is worth pursuing or maintaining. In other words, they should create a definable and realistic sales forecast.

STRATEGIES, TIPS & TECHNIQUES TO APPLY

Determining Realistic Revenue Streams and Related Goals

Accurately forecasting revenue streams requires salespeople listing their company's greatest strengths and weaknesses. This includes itemizing the specific strengths that competitors will find hard to compete with or various parts of the offering(s) that are hard to duplicate, as well as determining the most vulnerable aspects that could interfere with servicing the large account, such as slow decision making processes or being over extended in terms of resources or personnel.

Identifying potential yet realistic opportunities by referring back to identified future trends becomes a top priority. It is also essential to define all of the key individuals within the account, including champions, devil's advocates and resisters. If it becomes impossible to identify any of them, the process can still easily move forward by simply listing the names of the people the team considers to have the most weight and importance.

Defining a Revenue Target Goal

Identifying a revenue target goal is a two-step process that can be most effectively accomplished by first selecting an appropriate time frame for each specific revenue stream, which is typically extended out to a point that falls somewhere between one and three years into the future.

In the process it is important to determine what volume of revenue is achievable by the end of the identified time period. Volume can be measured in dollars, in the amount of products or services delivered, or in other quantifiable ways that the team as a whole finds applicable and acceptable. As volumes can be expected to vary depending on high or lower revenue target streams, high- and low-end revenue scenarios should be used as a basis for determining maximum and minimum performance indicators. (Times and dates can also be expected to vary depending upon high or minimum performance.)

In all cases, each separate goal needs to be quantitative in nature, while being stated from the large account's point of view rather than from the sales team's company.

Identify a Specific Goal for Each Paired Strength and Opportunity

Capitalizing on strengths and available opportunities while effectively pairing them in a creative way ultimately results in generating higher levels of revenue potential. It is important to recognize that the team may not be able to find a particular goal for each combined strength and opportunity. As similar goals might become appropriate for two or three different scenarios, goals may overlap. The main rationale behind completing the process is to obtain as much "usable" information as possible in order to weigh, dissect and measure it.

Validity Awareness and Assessment

Within the last portion of the process, it is essential to complete a validity assessment in order to ensure that all goals and strategies are compatible with one another and consistent with what the company is expected to deliver and/or maintain.

The validity assessment will help determine whether the main goal or particular secondary goals tend to aid or hinder the attainment of any revenue targets. It also allows team members to reassess determined timelines and streams of monetary return and to create a written format to show its generated statement of intent to the members of the large account.

The whole purpose of this exercise is to build a partnership with individual large accounts and associated members, show them just where the sales company wants to go with them, and how it plans to get there as cost effectively as possible.

POINTS TO PONDER — SOMETHING TO THINK ABOUT

1. Have you struggled with forecasting accurate revenue streams in the past? Why?
2. Why is it essential to create a realistic sales forecast?

TRAINING ACTIVITY — APPLICATION & ACTION PLAN

1. Develop a situational analysis for your account:
2. Based upon the concepts of this chapter determine realistic revenue streams and related goals for your situational analysis:
    a. Determine Realistic Revenue Streams and Related Goals
    b. Define a Revenue Target Goal
    c. Identify a Specific Goal for Each Paired Strength and Opportunity
    d. Validate Your Awareness and Assessment
3. Based upon the information you have collected and analyze, complete and compile your situational analysis.

About the Author

Timothy F. Bednarz, Ph.D. is CEO of the American Management Development Group, Inc. For over 20 years he has researched, designed and authored hundreds of learning and development programs used by Fortune 1000 companies.

He is also the author of *Great! What Makes Leaders Great. What They Did, How They Did It and What You Can Learn from It* (2011).

Speaking Availability

Timothy F. Bednarz, Ph.D. is available for speaking engagements for your next meeting or association event. He can be contacted at 800-654-4935 or by e-mail at timothy.bednarz@majorium.com.

Bulk Sales

Bulk sales of this book or any other titles available from Majorium Business Press. Inquiries can be directed to sales@majorium.com, or by phone at 800-6654-4935.

Quick Order Form

Fax orders: 715-342-1118. Send this form.

Telephone orders: Call 800-654-4935 toll-free. Have your credit card ready.

Email orders: sales@majorium.com

Postal orders: Majorium Business Press, 2025 Main Street, Stevens Point, WI 54481, USA.

Please send the following books:

____

____

____

____

Please send more FREE information on:

❑Catalog ❑Speaking/Seminars ❑Mailing Lists ❑Consulting

Name: ____

Address: ____

City: ____________________________ State: _____ Zip: __________

Telephone: ____

Email address: ____

Sales tax: Please add 5.5% for products shipped to Wisconsin addresses.

Shipping by air:

United States: $4.00 for first book and $2.00 for each additional product.

International: $9.00 for first book; $5.00 for each additional product (estimate).

Made in United States
Cleveland, OH
05 November 2026

47675525R00030